FROM THE EARTH
How Resources Are Made

HOW PRECIOUS METALS FORM

BY JULIA MCDONNELL

Gareth Stevens
PUBLISHING

Please visit our website, www.garethstevens.com. For a free color catalog of all our high-quality books, call toll free 1-800-542-2595 or fax 1-877-542-2596.

Library of Congress Cataloging-in-Publication Data

Names: McDonnell, Julia, 1979-
Title: How precious metals form / Julia McDonnell.
Description: New York : Gareth Stevens Publishing, [2017] | Series: From the
  earth: how resources are made | Includes index.
Identifiers: LCCN 2016015519 | ISBN 9781482447279 (pbk.) | ISBN 9781482447309 (library bound) | ISBN 9781482447293 (6 pack)
Subjects: LCSH: Precious metals–Juvenile literature. | Mines and mineral
  resources–Juvenile literature.
Classification: LCC TS729 .M33 2017 | DDC 622/.342–dc23
LC record available at https://lccn.loc.gov/2016015519

Published in 2017 by
Gareth Stevens Publishing
111 East 14th Street, Suite 349
New York, NY 10003

Copyright © 2017 Gareth Stevens Publishing

Designer: Laura Bowen
Editor: Therese Shea

Photo credits: Cover, pp. 1–32 (title bar) Dimec/Shutterstock.com; cover, pp. 1–32 (text box) mattasbestos/Shutterstock.com; cover, pp. 1–32 (background) Alina G/Shutterstock.com; cover, p. 1 (gold) studiocasper/Getty Images; p. 5 (main) DEA/De Agostini/Getty Images; p. 5 (inset) MarcelClemens/Shutterstock.com; p. 7 (periodic table) charobnica/Shutterstock.com; p. 7 (ruthenium diagram) BlueRingMedia/Shutterstock.com; pp. 7 (ruthenium photo), 13 (rhodium and rhenium), 14 (osmium and platinum) Alchemist-hp/Wikimedia Commons; p. 8 Andrey N Bannov/Shutterstock.com; p. 9 Lemaire Stephane/Getty Images; p. 11 (main) Science Photo Library - Mehau Kulyk/Brand X Pictures/Getty Images; pp. 11 (inset), 12 (moon and mars) courtesy of NASA.com; p. 13 (palladium) Stats1995/Wikimedia Commons; p. 15 (Earth) seveniwe/Shutterstock.com; p. 15 (borehole) Insider/Wikimedia Commons; p. 17 (main) EuTuga/Wikimedia Commons; p. 17 (inset) Materialscientist/Wikimedia Commons; p. 19 kaband/Shutterstock.com; p. 21 John W Banagan/Getty Images; p. 22 Anthony Bradshaw/Getty Images; p. 25 (main) Garry Adams/Getty Images; p. 25 (inset) My name is boy/Shutterstock.com; p. 27 Hulton Archive/Getty Images; p. 29 kubais/Shutterstock.com.

Printed in the United States of America

CPSIA compliance information: Batch #CS16GS: For further information contact Gareth Stevens, New York, New York at 1-800-542-2595.

CONTENTS

A Very Natural Resource 4

What Are the Precious Metals? 6

Where Did They Come From? 10

Kinds of Deposits 16

Why Is Ore Important? 18

How Are They Mined? 20

How Are They Used? 24

You Decide 26

Part of the Past...and Future 28

Glossary 30

For More Information 31

Index 32

Words in the glossary appear in **bold** type the first time they are used in the text.

A VERY NATURAL RESOURCE

Shiny. Expensive. Fancy. Are these the words that come to mind when you think about gold and silver? They may fit, but there's much more to these **substances** than just how pretty they look or how much they're worth. Gold and silver belong to the group known as precious metals. Precious metals are naturally occurring metallic elements that are rare and have a high value.

Though people have created art, economies, and scientific breakthroughs based on these materials, precious metals have the most natural source possible: our Earth. The ways we collect, prepare, and use them affect our lives and planet.

GOLD ABOVE ALL

When it comes to being considered valuable, gold has been a desirable metal for centuries. And that's not just because it's rare or pretty to look at. It doesn't **corrode**, burn, or **react**. It's safe to handle and melts at a temperature that's easy for people to produce.

ancient Egyptian
burial mask
of King Tut

gold

Though gold in nature can be found as flakes and grains, a nugget like the one shown here is probably what most people picture.

WHAT ARE THE PRECIOUS METALS?

Gold and silver may be the most well-known, but platinum, rhodium, palladium, osmium, iridium, rhenium, and ruthenium are also precious metals. Just as with any form of matter, their smallest possible unit is an atom—and it's what's inside each atom that makes each metal **unique**.

At the center of each atom is a nucleus made up of neutrons (**particles** with no charge) and protons (particles with a positive charge). Electrons (negatively charged particles) circle the nucleus. Each element has a different number of protons in its atoms, which gives it its atomic number. The higher the number, the more protons there are, and the heavier the element is.

IT'S ELEMENTARY

Each precious metal is found on a chart called the periodic table of elements with its own two-letter symbol and atomic number: ruthenium (Ru, 44), rhodium (Rh, 45), palladium (Pd, 46), rhenium (Re, 75), osmium (Os, 76), iridium (Ir, 77), platinum (Pt, 78), silver (Ag, 47), and gold (Au, 79).

Periodic Table of Elements

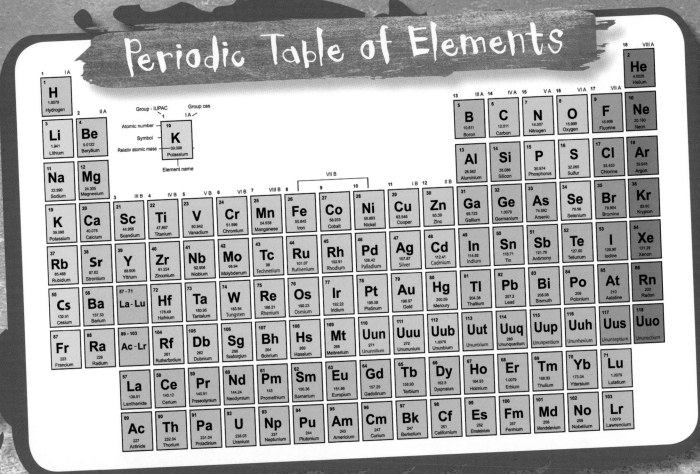

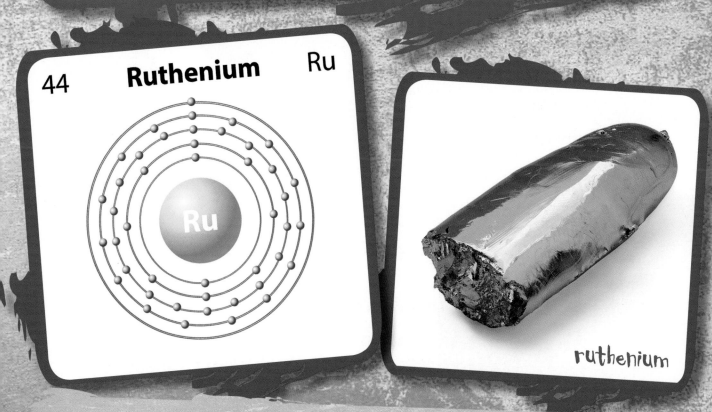

Ruthenium

44   **Ruthenium**   Ru

ruthenium

This picture of a ruthenium atom shows 44 electrons circling around the nucleus, which contains its protons and neutrons.

Most precious metals belong in the group called noble metals. That means they resist **oxidation** and don't corrode. Most are ductile, meaning they can be stretched without breaking, and malleable, meaning they can be pressed and rolled into thin sheets. Precious metals usually have luster, too. That means they reflect light, making them look shiny.

Precious metals are also transition metals, or metals whose atoms bond easily with those of other elements because of the arrangement of their electrons. Precious metals conduct electricity as well, so they're in demand for making parts for electronic and scientific **equipment**. In addition to all these valuable features, a metal's rarity also makes it "precious."

molten gold

MAGIC . . . OR SCIENCE?

If you can't find or afford gold, why not try to make it? In the Middle Ages, people tried—and failed—to do just that. They experimented with cheaper metals, often combining them with other substances and liquids. They didn't make gold, but what they learned from this work contributed to the study of chemistry.

The royal gate at France's Versailles palace is covered with 100,000 pieces of gold leaf, which is gold beaten into extremely thin sheets.

9

WHERE DID THEY COME FROM?

Precious metals found in Earth are actually older than the planet itself! According to one idea, the formation process began about 4.6 billion years ago. The solar system was just a cloud of dust and gases then, full of matter that became the building blocks of the planets.

Something—perhaps a nearby exploding star—created waves, sort of like ripples in a pond. The waves caused the cloud to **collapse** and form a spinning disk. As it spun, it grew hotter, and the matter within it became dense, or tightly packed together. Atoms of the gases hydrogen and helium fused to create great energy—and our sun!

DUST ON DISPLAY

Do you want to see some space dust? Look no farther than Saturn's rings. Scientists think they may be "leftovers" from Saturn's formation. They may also be bits of moons, asteroids, and other space objects that were ripped apart by Saturn's gravity. The matter in the dust cloud might have looked something like the matter in the rings.

This picture of a star explosion, called a supernova, shows how the waves of energy that are created move outward and affect everything around it.

Saturn

After the sun was formed, the force of gravity bound bits of particles together, forming larger and larger masses. At the same time, solar winds cleared lighter materials such as gases. Close to the sun, rocky and metallic dust combined to create the four **terrestrial** planets that could withstand the nearby sun's heat: Mercury, Venus, Earth, and Mars. Moons, **comets**, asteroids, and other space rocks formed as well.

Farther from the sun, where solar winds and heat had less effect, gaseous and icy material formed the planets we call gas giants: Jupiter, Saturn, Uranus, and Neptune.

moon

Mars

Could the moon and Mars be sources of precious metals for us someday? Rocky samples taken from the surfaces of both reveal gold, platinum, and palladium.

HOW WERE THEY NAMED?

PRECIOUS METAL	NAME COMES FROM	WHICH MEANS
ruthenium	Latin *Ruthenia*	Russia
rhodium	Greek *rhodon*	rose
palladium	Greek *Pallas*	name for Greek goddess Athena
rhenium	Latin *Rhenus*	Rhine River
osmium	Greek *osme*	smell
iridium	Greek *iris*	rainbow
platinum	Spanish *platina*	little silver
silver	Old English *seolfor*	silver
gold	Old English *geolu*	yellow

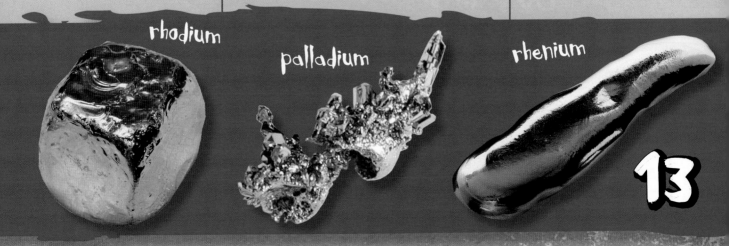

rhodium

palladium

rhenium

13

When Earth formed, it was so hot it was likely at least partly molten, or melted. Dense matter sank toward the planet's core, or center, and that included metals. Lighter matter rose to Earth's surface. When the planet cooled, its precious metals were trapped in its inner layers, where we currently don't have the **technology** to reach them.

We can reach precious metals in the crust, however. So where did these come from? Scientists think they probably reached Earth when asteroids crashed onto the surface. Some of these asteroids may have been hundreds of miles wide.

osmium

platinum

BURIED TREASURE

Precious metals are siderophile elements. The word "siderophile" comes from Greek words that together mean "iron-loving." The metals probably sank toward Earth's iron-rich core as the planet formed. There are much greater amounts of these metals in Earth's core and mantle than on its crust.

Earth's layers

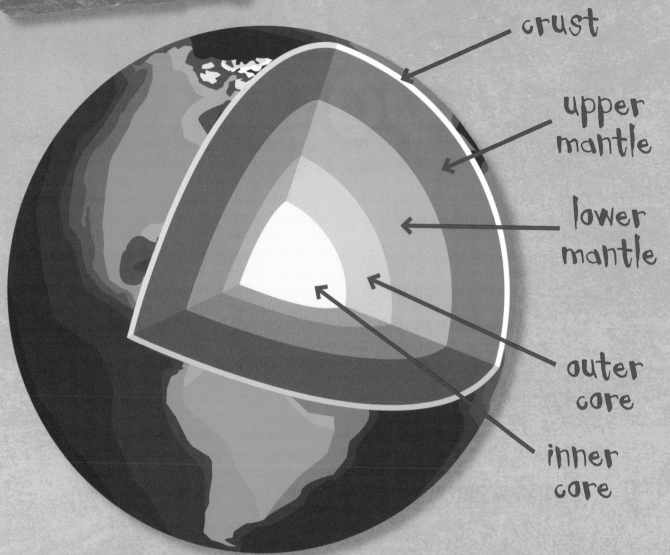

crust

upper mantle

lower mantle

outer core

inner core

Kola Superdeep Borehole site

Earth's crust is only 3 to 25 miles (4.8 to 40 km) thick, but no one has dug far enough to reach the mantle. The deepest drilling attempt is the Kola Superdeep Borehole in Russia: only 9 inches (23 cm) in diameter, but over 7.5 miles (12 km) deep.

Kinds of Deposits

Precious metals are found on every continent—even Antarctica. Some precious metals are found in pure form. Others occur as **alloys**, either naturally or man-made.

Sometimes precious metals are found in lode deposits. These are veins or cracks within or between rocks filled with a metal. They're also discovered in placer deposits. These are pockets of metals that have been removed from another area by weathering. That means the bits are swept to a new location by the forces of water or wind. Placer deposits may be found in the form of nuggets or harder-to-spot flakes and grains.

Making Metals Even Better

Alloys often combine the best qualities of substances. For example, silver easily tarnishes, or becomes dull or discolored. However, when copper is added to silver, it becomes sterling silver, which is used for medical tools and musical instruments. Gold is soft. However, when it's mixed with copper, the alloy is strong enough to be jewelry.

iridium

The precious metal iridium has been found in a layer of rock that dates back to 65 million years ago—when the dinosaurs died out! Scientists are trying to find out if this is the remains of a giant asteroid that brought the iridium to the planet.

WHY IS ORE IMPORTANT?

A major source of precious metals is ore, and mining companies depend on it. Ore is a kind of rock that contains enough metal to make it valuable for companies to collect it. An ore deposit can hold several different elements. Silver is often discovered with lead and zinc, and gold can be found with copper and silver.

Once the ore has been removed from the crust, it's treated so the variety of minerals can be separated. Sometimes a precious metal is obtained when another substance is being processed. For example, rhenium is left after copper has been mined.

FROZEN METALS?

When Earth was much younger, its continents were one landmass. So, not surprisingly, Antarctica has precious metals like the other six continents. But ice-covered ground, a freezing cold climate, and long periods of darkness make it a tough place to live and work. In 1988, the Antarctic Treaty protected the continent's environment by banning "any activity relating to mineral resources."

It looks like these mining vehicles are loading useless rocks—but valuable metals are hiding in that ore!

19

HOW ARE THEY MINED?

Once ore is located, there are several ways to reach it. Surface mining involves drilling or blasting rocks with explosives. The rocks are hauled away, and the metal is removed. Surface mining may also mean digging large pits and removing the ore inside.

When the ore is farther down, underground mining is the answer. Tunnels are dug, sometimes over 1 mile (1.6 km) deep. Ore is cut, blasted, or drilled into pieces and carried to the mine's opening.

Sometimes ore is found in water. High-powered hoses are used to break apart the ore. Special machines then suck up the pieces, which are later sorted.

STAY AWAY!

Once a mine is no longer in use, what happens? Some people falsely think it's a safe place to explore. There are dangers from rocks, tunnels, water, old equipment, and gases. Animals look for shelter in old mines and may get trapped. The creatures themselves (such as bears and snakes) can be dangerous.

This gold mine in Australia shows how surface mining is done in layers.

21

Once the ore is ready to be processed, it's usually crushed so the precious metals within it are more exposed. The next step is extraction, which means the metal is separated from other matter that isn't needed, such as rock, minerals, and other metals. Next comes refining.

Refining removes **impurities** from metals. The precious metals might be usable as they are, but they could be more useful or valuable in an even purer form. Depending on the type of metal, there are several ways to refine precious metal ore. Processes use heat, chemicals, magnets, water, or electricity.

DON'T THROW THAT OUT!

Just like glass and paper can be recycled, precious metals can have a second life. Whether a pair of gold earrings or a part from a computer, this metal can be used again. The metals are extracted with methods similar to how they were originally obtained and sold to businesses that turn them into other products.

melting
scrap gold

METAL REFINING PROCESSES

Floatation

Ore is placed in a **solution** of water and chemicals. Metal sticks to air bubbles and rises to the surface.

Smelting

Ore is placed in high temperatures. Unwanted matter is burned off or separated from the metal.

Electrowinning

Ore is placed in a solution. Electricity is passed through the solution. The metal separates from other substances.

Magnetic Separation

Ore is exposed to a special magnet. The magnet attracts the metal and separates it from other substances.

Chemical Separation

Ore is placed in a chemical solution. The metal is separated from other substances or dissolved. The metal is taken out.

23

HOW ARE THEY USED?

With their natural shine and color, precious metals have been celebrated through the centuries for their beauty and used to show wealth, especially in jewelry, fashion, and art.

Precious metals have been used as money, too. They've been made into coins. They're also a way for countries to store wealth, usually in the form of gold or silver bars called bullion.

Precious metals are also used in medicines, dental fillings, cancer treatments, and medical tools. And in technology, they can be found in anything from tiny circuit breakers to parts for huge vehicles. Precious metals even "return" to space in spacecraft!

BASIC BASES

Elements such as copper, lead, iron, zinc, nickel, and tin are more abundant in Earth's crust and therefore cheaper. These are called base metals and are just as essential as precious metals. They're used in construction, vehicle parts, electrical wires, batteries, and electronics. They're also needed to make the important alloys steel and bronze.

silver

Medical creams containing silver, seen here, are used to heal burns and fight infections.

In the past, precious metals, especially silver and gold, were used to make coins.

YOU DECIDE

Mining precious metals is **controversial**. Water, soil, and air can be polluted with chemicals used in the mining and refining of metals. Land is dug up by large machinery, forests are cut down, and animals lose their homes. Sometimes conditions are dangerous for workers, too.

However, mining also means jobs as well as money for education and health services. Precious metals can improve lives through technology and medical advances. When mining companies care for their workers as well as the environment, communities can flourish.

Do you think precious metals are important enough to continue mining? How should mining practices be changed in the future?

CAN GOLD TRANSFORM A COUNTRY?

When gold was found near Sacramento, California, in 1848, the territory had fewer than 1,000 American citizens living there. Less than 2 years later, 100,000 people had arrived in hopes of striking it rich. People from around the world moved to booming new towns as the mining industry grew, displacing Native Americans from their traditional lands. California soon became a state.

People swarmed to the rivers of California to make their fortunes, especially in 1849. They were labeled '49ers.

PART OF THE PAST... AND FUTURE

Earth's available supply of precious metals won't last forever, even if we explore possible new sources of ore such as Antarctica or the ocean floor. Scientists are now finding ways to make synthetic, or man-made, precious metals. However, the process can cost more than the metals themselves! Scientists will keep trying though, because precious metals help advance science through both their use as tools and as materials in experiments.

Precious metals have been an essential part of Earth's history as well as humankind's. They'll definitely remain a part of our future, too.

NO LONGER PRECIOUS

Lighter and shinier than silver, the aluminum that makes up common objects such as soda cans and airplanes used to be more precious than gold! Though plentiful in Earth's crust, it was costly to extract from its ore. However, technology made that possible in 1886. Soon widely available, aluminum's price dropped.

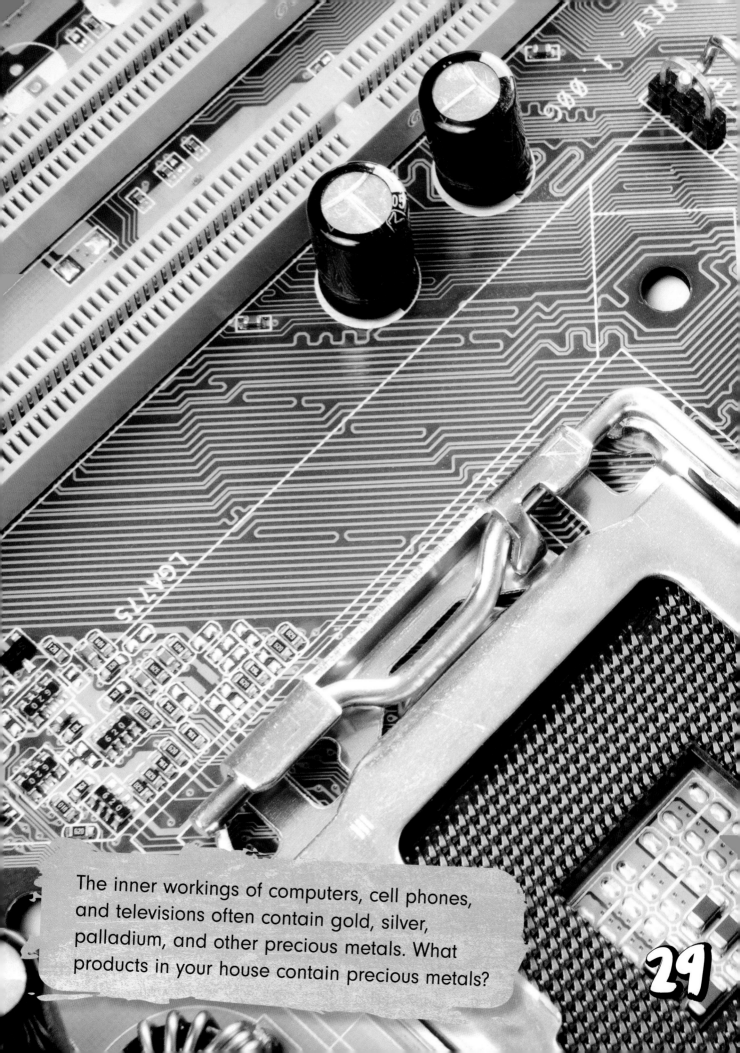

The inner workings of computers, cell phones, and televisions often contain gold, silver, palladium, and other precious metals. What products in your house contain precious metals?

GLOSSARY

alloy: matter made of two or more metals, or a metal and a nonmetal, melted together

collapse: to break apart and fall down suddenly

comet: an object in outer space that develops a long, bright tail when it passes near the sun

controversial: causing arguments

corrode: to slowly break apart and destroy a metal through a chemical process

environment: the natural world

equipment: tools, clothing, and other items needed for a job

impurity: something unwanted that is mixed in with a substance

oxidation: the process of combining with oxygen

particle: one of the tiny building blocks of matter

react: to change after coming in contact with another substance

solution: a mixture

substance: a matter or material

technology: the way people do something using tools and the tools that they use

terrestrial: relating to land

unique: one of a kind

FOR MORE INFORMATION

BOOKS

Hawking, Lucy, and Stephen Hawking. *George and the Big Bang.* New York, NY: Simon & Schuster Books for Young Readers, 2012.

Raum, Elizabeth. *The Story Behind Gold.* Chicago, IL: Heinemann Library, 2008.

Schwartz, Alvin. *Gold and Silver, Silver and Gold: Tales of Hidden Treasure.* New York, NY: Farrar, Straus and Giroux, 2009.

WEBSITES

Chem4Kids
www.chem4kids.com
Find facts about each of the precious metals.

Geology for Kids: Gold
kidsgeo.com/geology-for-kids/0029B-gold.php
Learn how gold is found in nature.

INDEX

alloys 16, 24

aluminum 28

asteroids 10, 12, 14, 17

atom 6, 7, 8, 10

atomic number 6

base metals 24

core 14

crust 14, 15, 18, 24, 28

electrons 6, 7, 8

extraction 22, 28

gold 4, 5, 6, 8, 9, 12, 13, 16,
    18, 21, 22, 24, 25, 26,
    28, 29

impurities 22

iridium 6, 13, 17

jobs 26

Kola Superdeep Borehole 15

lode deposits 16

mantle 14, 15

neutrons 6, 7

noble metals 8

nucleus 6, 7

ore 18, 19, 20, 22, 23, 28

osmium 6, 13

palladium 6, 12, 13, 29

placer deposits 16

platinum 6, 12, 13

pollution 26

protons 6, 7

refining 22, 23, 26

rhenium 6, 13, 18

rhodium 6, 13

ruthenium 6, 7, 13

siderophile elements 14

silver 4, 6, 13, 16, 18, 24, 25,
    28, 29

surface mining 20, 21, 26

transition metals 8

underground mining 20, 26

uses 24